# The Little Prince

Antoine de Saint-Exupery

# TEACHER GUIDE

**NOTE:**

The trade book edition of the novel used to prepare this guide is found in the Novel Units catalog and on the Novel Units website. Using other editions may have varied page references.

Please note: We have assigned Interest Levels based on our knowledge of the themes and ideas of the books included in the Novel Units sets, however, please assess the appropriateness of this novel or trade book for the age level and maturity of your students prior to reading with them. You know your students best!

**ISBN 978-1-58130-718-4**

To order, contact your local school supply store, or:

Toll-Free Fax: 877.716.7272
Phone: 888.650.4224
3901 Union Blvd., Suite 155
St. Louis, MO 63115

sales@novelunits.com

**novelunits.com**

# Table of Contents

# Skills and Strategies

## Thinking
Research, compare/contrast, analysis, brainstorming, critical thinking

## Writing
Journal response, poetry, prose, epilogue, letter

## Vocabulary
Target words, definitions, application

## Across the Curriculum
Art—drawing, caricature, collage

## Literary Elements
Characterization, irony, personification, simile, metaphor, allusion, fable, allegory, theme, universality, foreshadowing

## Comprehension
Predicting, cause/effect, inference

## Listening/Speaking
Discussion, oral reading, poetry reading, film viewing, music

**Genre:** fiction; fable/allegory

**Setting:** Sahara Desert, Africa

**Date:** written in 1943

**Point-of-View:** first person

**Themes:** friendship, love, innocence, loyalty

**Protagonist:** the Little Prince

**Antagonist:** the Little Prince's inner search

**Style:** narrative

## Summary

The narrator, a pilot, is downed in the Sahara Desert, and attempts to repair his wrecked plane. He encounters a small apparition, the Little Prince, who asks him to draw a sheep. Their ensuing dialogue reveals the conflict that led the Little Prince to leave his own planet and the details of his journey from planet to planet until his arrival on Earth. The friendship that develops between the pilot and the Little Prince and the Little Prince's encounter with a fox help him discover the secret of what is important in life. The story is a study in contrasts: reality/unreality; childhood/adulthood; joy/sadness; life/death.

## Historical Background

Written in the midst of World War II, *The Little Prince* portrays problems that Saint-Exupéry and his native France were facing. France was occupied by the Nazis, and the author grieved over the suffering of his family, his friends, and his countrymen. The drawing of the boa constrictor swallowing an elephant depicts the political monster that was swallowing Europe.

## Characters

**The Little Prince:** visitor to earth, probably from Asteroid B-612, who leaves his flower, the love of his life, in search of the value and importance of life; loves sunsets and thinks grown-ups are strange and confuse everything

**His flower:** his friend and companion whom he faithfully tends, yet leaves because of her vanity. Note the duality of her character: beauty/vanity; causes happiness/pain; cause of the Little Prince's departure from/return to his planet; essential to development of the tale

# The Little Prince's Encounters on Earth

**The narrator:** a pilot who is attempting to repair his downed airplane; becomes friend and confidant of the Little Prince

**The snake:** the first creature he meets on earth; symbolizes death

**The roses:** reveal the identity of his flower

**The fox:** teaches the Little Prince what is really important in life; symbolizes friendship

**The railway switchman:** reveals basic (adult) dissatisfaction with life

**The merchant:** interested only in saving time

# The Little Prince's Interplanetary Encounters

*Note:* Each character symbolizes some futile aspect of adult existence, and all except the lamplighter are completely self-absorbed.

**The king:** believes he rules over everything and issues demands that ensure absolute obedience

**The conceited man:** refuses to hear anything but praise

**The tippler:** ironically drinks to forget his shame over drinking

**The businessman:** a picture of futility; counting, recounting, and banking "his stars"

**The lamplighter:** never rests because he must continually light and re-light his lamp

**The geographer:** records only things that are "matters of consequence"; never explores for himself but depends on others' efficiency

# About the Author

Antoine de Saint-Exupéry was born June 29, 1900, in Lyon, France. He was educated in Jesuit schools and at the Villa Saint Jean in Frebourg, Switzerland. He joined the French Air Force, serving as a mechanic, in 1921. In 1926, he left the Air Force to become a commercial pilot, flying mail routes over North Africa and South America. In 1935, he was stranded in the desert after crashing his plane. He flew to many South African cities during the Spanish Civil War. He married Consuelo Suncion in 1931.

In 1938, after German troops occupied France, Saint-Exupéry moved to the United States and flew dangerous missions over the Mediterranean Sea and the Sahara Desert. In 1942, he joined the American army, serving as a pilot, but later returned to his old French Army squadron in North Africa. On July 31, 1944, he flew his last mission. German airplanes destroyed his plane over the Mediterranean.

Saint-Exupéry based his first novel, *Courrier,* on his experiences flying mail routes. First published in French in 1928, it was translated into English as *Southern Mail,* in 1933. Other works include *Vol de Nuit (Night Flight),* 1931; *Terre des Hommes (Wind, Sand, and Stars),* 1939; *Pilote de Guerre (Flight to Arras),* 1942; *Lettre a un Otage (Letter to a Hostage),* 1943; *Wartime Writings, 1939-1944, Citadelle (Wisdom of the Sands),* posthumous.

# Pre-reading Glossary

Place the following words on the overhead transparency and have students write the meanings.

1. **Metaphor:** comparison of two objects, not indicating the resemblance with "like" or "as"; can be a single isolated comparison or an extended allegory

2. **Simile:** comparison of two objects, joined by an indicator of resemblance such as "like" or "as"

3. **Allegory:** a form of extended metaphor in which objects, persons, and actions are equated with meanings outside the narrative itself; such meanings may be religious, moral, political, personal, or satiric

4. **Fable:** a tale, either in prose or verse, told to teach a moral

5. **Personification:** a figure of speech that endows animals, ideas, abstractions, and inanimate forms with human characteristics

6. **Universality:** the presence in a piece of writing of an appeal to all readers of all time; e.g., characters' portrayal of emotions such as love or jealousy

# Initiating Activities

Use one or more of the following suggestions to establish an appropriate mindset for the novel.

1. Note the importance of the book's dedication to Leon Werth and present the following information: Werth was a French essayist, novelist, and art critic. He and Saint-Exupéry met in 1931. Although opposite in political views and religious backgrounds, and in spite of Werth's twenty-two year age seniority, the two became close friends. Werth spent the war years in France "hungry and cold." After World War II ended, Werth said, "Peace, without Tonio (Exupéry) isn't entirely peace."
   Source: **http://littleprince.8m.com/werth.html**

2. Place the title, *The Little Prince,* on an overhead transparency. Elicit student responses from those who have read the book, those who have heard about the book, those who have seen the movie, etc.

3. Place the following quote from Saint-Exupéry on the overhead transparency: "There is no hope of joy except in human relations." Elicit student response and discuss.

4. Place a drawing patterned after the author's picture of a boa constrictor digesting an elephant. Ask students to write down what they see in the picture. Discuss responses.

## Teaching Approaches

1. The novel can be approached as a fable in which the prince is sent to earth to teach the narrator (pilot) and his readers what is really important in life. He is assisted by parodies of men who are consumed with the futility of searching for the meaning of life in the wrong ways, inanimate objects (flower and the baobabs), and animals (the fox and the snake). The fable takes place in a world where the supernatural, i.e., interplanetary travel and talking animals, exists. The Little Prince is the protagonist who leaves his home, ventures into a new world, and presumably returns home wiser and more content. He learns a valuable lesson about friendship from the fox and the lesson of dying from the snake. The Prince then teaches these lessons to the narrator (pilot). Through the Little Prince's friendship and encouragement, the pilot discovers the importance of friendship, love, and loyalty.

2. When viewed as a book for teenagers and adults, the book can be presented as an allegory. Certain characters represent a particular concept. Allegorical figures include the narrator: adult who opens his heart to friendship; the Little Prince: childhood innocence lost and found; the rose: love; the fox: friendship; the snake: death.

3. When viewed as a book with autobiographical content, Saint-Exupéry, a pilot, was stranded when his plane crashed in the desert in 1935, and he experienced the trauma of being without water. The Little Prince is possibly patterned after Saint-Exupéry's younger brother, François, who died when he was a child. The rose, whom the Little Prince loves deeply, is a compilation of the two women to whom Saint-Exupéry was closest. His wife, Consuelo, was quite beautiful. They experienced friction and separation during their marriage, due in part to the differences in their lifestyles. The other was his mother, from whom he was separated when he was away at boarding school. In addition, the rose may portray some characteristics of Saint-Exupéry's friend, Leon Werth, to whom he dedicated the novel. They were close friends who were separated because of the war.

## Attribute Web

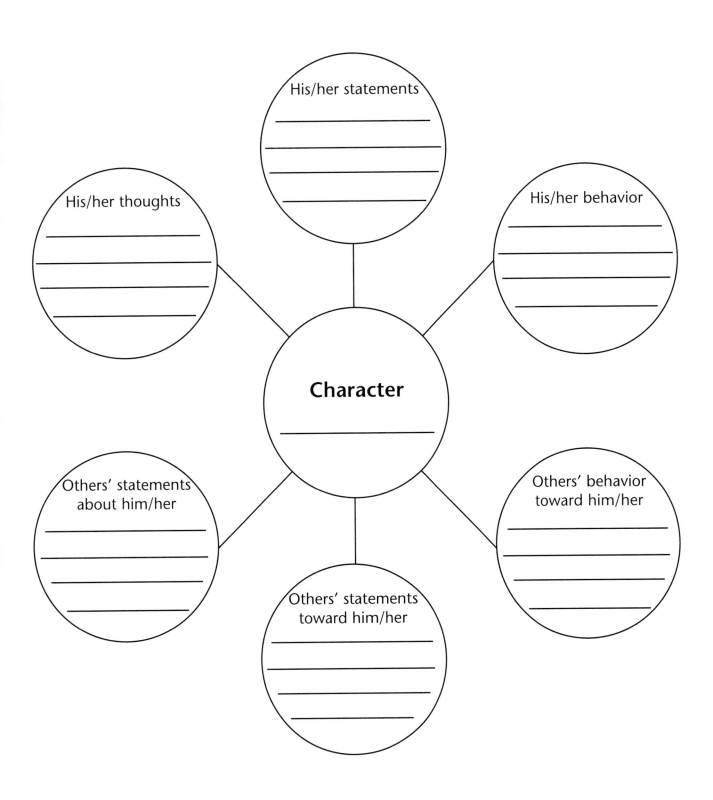

His/her statements

His/her thoughts

His/her behavior

**Character**

Others' statements about him/her

Others' statements toward him/her

Others' behavior toward him/her

# Character Analysis

**Directions:** List some of the characters who appear in the novel in the boxes below. Begin the chart after reading the first six chapters and add to the chart as you continue reading the novel. Working in small groups, discuss the attributes of the various characters with other members of your group. In each character's box, write several words or phrases you feel describe that character.

# Character Attribute Chart

**Directions:** Choose at least five characters from the book. List their names in the left-hand boxes. Fill in the other boxes with requested information.

| Character | One-Word Description | Appearance | Significance to the Story | Do you know anyone similar? |
|---|---|---|---|---|
| | | | | |
| | | | | |
| | | | | |
| | | | | |
| | | | | |
| | | | | |
| | | | | |

# Story Map

**Directions:** Use the diagram below with a partner or small group to free associate thoughts about the novel after you have finished reading it. Jot down your thoughts in a similar format on a large piece of paper.

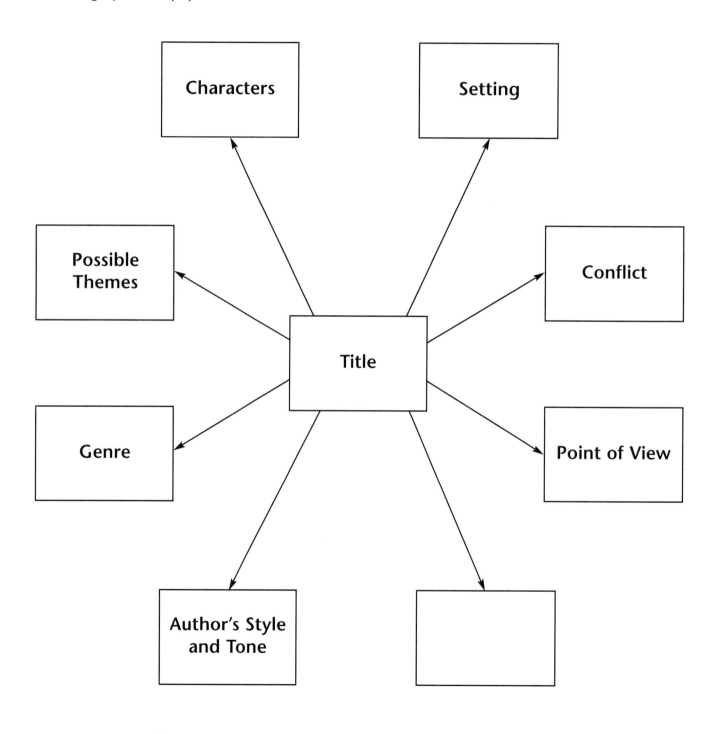

# Cause/Effect Chart

**Directions:** Make a flow chart to show decisions a character made, the decisions (s)he could have made, and the result(s) of each. (Use your imagination to speculate on the results of decisions the character could have made.)

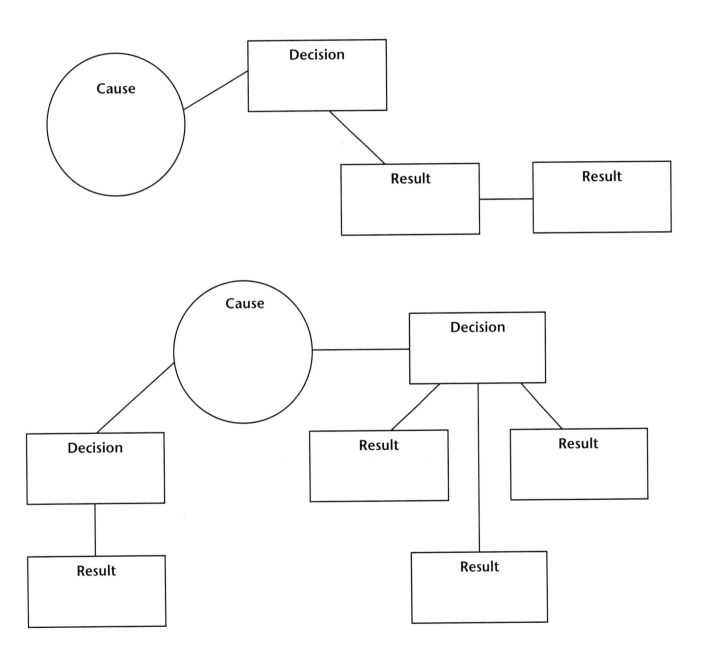

# Chapters 1-2, pp. 3-10

The narrator, a pilot who is attempting to repair his plane in the Sahara Desert, meets the Little Prince, who asks him to draw a sheep.

## Vocabulary

| | | | |
|---|---|---|---|
| primeval (3) | pondered (3) | consequence (5) | intimately (5) |
| apparition (6) | cumbersome (9) | indulgently (9) | |

## Discussion Questions

1. Read Chapter 1 aloud. Make prior arrangements for a student to read aloud Robert Frost's "The Road Not Taken." Discuss the narrator's desire to become an artist and his comment, "So then I chose another profession, and learned to pilot airplanes." Compare Frost's "road less traveled by" with the "road" the narrator has taken and discuss whether or not he feels he made the right choice. (*Responses will vary. Note that both of the professions [artist and pilot] were, at that time, roads "less traveled." While Frost apparently is pleased with his choice [between English teacher and poet], he realizes that toward the end of his life, he may regret not going back and traveling the other road. The narrator wanted to become an artist, but, because grown-ups did not understand, he becomes a pilot. Hints of his regret occur throughout the novel. pp. 3-6)*

2. Compare/contrast grown-ups and children's views of "matters of consequence" (pp. 5, 8). (*Responses will vary. Elicit student response about the priorities of adults compared with those of teenagers today.*)

3. Discuss the appearance of the Little Prince, his request, and its effect on the narrator (a pilot). (*The pilot faces a life and death situation in the Sahara Desert and must repair his downed plane. He feels isolated and alone until he is astonished by the appearance of the Little Prince, who asks the narrator to draw him a sheep. This request triggers memories of the narrator's feelings of inadequacies as an artist, but the Little Prince is delighted with the finished product. pp. 6-10)*

## Supplementary Activities

1. Have students analyze the drawing of the Little Prince and begin a list of facts about him. Continue this as the story progresses. (*for example, extraordinarily small person, wears boots and is dressed in a long coat with stars on shoulders, carries sword, lives where everything is small, imaginative, etc. pp. 6-10)*

2. Have students respond in their journals to the Little Prince's statement, "That is exactly the way I wanted it!" (p. 10) in response to the pilot's drawing of a box for the sheep.

3. Place the word "isolation" on an overhead transparency. Elicit student response to different types of isolation and times they have felt completely isolated. Analyze the simile, "I was more isolated than a shipwrecked sailor on a raft in the middle of the ocean" (p. 6).

# Chapters 3-4, pp. 10-19

The pilot discovers that the Little Prince is from a very small planet. This section contrasts grown-ups and children.

## Vocabulary

| | | | |
|---|---|---|---|
| peal (11) | impenetrable (11) | reverie (11) | contemplation (12) |
| asteroid (13) | astronomer (14) | forbearance (17) | |

## Discussion Questions

1. Discuss clues to the Little Prince's identity and the pilot's response to him. (*He is from a very small planet, probably Asteroid B-612, which is scarcely any larger than a house. The pilot and the Little Prince become friends. pp. 10-15*)

2. Examine the author's comparison/contrast of grown-ups and children. Ask students if they agree or disagree. (*grown-ups: unimaginative, impressed with style and elegance, love facts and figures, fail to understand life; children: imaginative, concerned with essential matters such as what a person's voice sounds like and what games he enjoys, the beauty of things instead of the cost, the belief in existence of imaginary people and things. pp. 15-17*)

## Supplementary Activities

1. Have students continue to list facts about the Little Prince.

2. Based on the statement, "For those who understand life, figures are a matter of indifference" (p. 17), have students write in their journals what it means to understand life.

3. Analyze the universality of the statement, "I like my misfortunes to be taken seriously" (p. 11).

# Chapters 5-7, pp. 19-31

The Little Prince reveals the catastrophe of the baobabs (plants) on his planet and his love for his flower.

## Vocabulary

| | | | |
|---|---|---|---|
| catastrophe (19) | inoffensively (21) | tedious (23) | moralist (23) |
| naïve (28) | moment (31) | blundering (31) | |

## Discussion Questions

1. Discuss the catastrophe of the baobabs. Read the description and examine and describe the message in the drawing on page 25. Brainstorm with students about environmental issues that threaten today's world. Correlate with the adage, "Never put off until tomorrow what you can do today." (*The baobabs are bad plants that grow as tall as trees and eventually split the planet into pieces. The only way to nullify their destructive nature is to destroy them when they are very small. Environmental issues could range from noxious weeds that destroy crops to raging forest fires. pp. 20-24*)

2. Examine evidence of the Little Prince's homesickness. *(He misses his sunsets, keeps thinking he is at home, and is concerned that his sheep might eat his flower. pp. 24-31)*

3. Analyze the developing relationship between the pilot and the Little Prince. Note the pilot's reaction to the prince's distress. *(As the pilot learns more about the secrets of the prince's "sad little life," their friendship deepens. The prince accuses the pilot of talking and acting like a grown-up, and the pilot realizes how unimportant his own needs are when faced with the prince's deep distress. He takes the Little Prince into his arms and comforts him. pp. 27-31)*

## Supplementary Activities

1. Have students continue to list facts about the Little Prince.

2. Based on the phrase, "It is such a secret place, the land of tears" (p. 31), have students write a five-senses poem about "sorrow." Pattern—Line 1: color of the emotion; Line 2: sound of the emotion; Line 3: taste of the emotion; Line 4: smell of the emotion; Line 5: sight (what the emotion looks like); Line 6: feeling evoked by the emotion. This can be done individually or as a class.

3. Have students draw a caricature illustrating the metaphor "...he is not a man—he is a mushroom!" (p. 29)

# Chapters 8-9, pp. 31-40

The Little Prince reveals more about his flower: his love and tender care for her, her vanity and demands, his regrets in his failure to understand her, and the circumstances of their separation.

## Vocabulary

| | | | |
|---|---|---|---|
| coquettish (33) | abashed (33) | vanity (33) | complex (35) |
| stratagems (37) | extinct (38) | | |

## Discussion Questions

1. Analyze the relationship between the Little Prince and his rose. Correlate with human response to falling in love: the initial "rose-colored glasses" stage, facing the reality of human fallibility, failure to understand needs of the other, decision to leave, regrets, and so forth. *(She first comes into his life as a tiny seed that grows into an object of beauty. He cares for her gently and unselfishly but begins to be distressed and confused by her vanity and deceit. Only when he prepares to leave does she realize his value and attempt to make amends. After he leaves, he regrets his failure to understand her and grieves for her. pp. 31-40)*

2. Discuss the Little Prince's preparations for leaving his planet and what this reveals about him. *(He puts his planet in perfect order, cleaning out the volcanoes and pulling up remaining shoots of baobabs. He waters his flower and prepares to place his rose under the protective glass globe. These actions reveal that he is meticulous and compassionate. pp. 38-40)*

3. Brainstorm with students the significance of the Little Prince's statement, "I was too young to know how to love her..." (p. 37). *(Responses will vary.)*

## Supplementary Activities

1. Analyze the literary devices: **Personification**—the rose: "She chose...she dressed," etc. (p. 32)
   **Similes**—Volcanic eruptions are like fires in a chimney (p. 38).

2. Correlate the statement, "I ought to have judged by deeds and not by words" (p. 36) with the adage, "Actions speak louder than words." Have students write a journal response in which they relate a time they should have followed this advice.

# Chapters 10-12, pp. 41-52

The pilot relates details about the Little Prince's interplanetary travels. The reader is introduced to the king, the conceited man, and the tippler.

## Vocabulary

| | | | |
|---|---|---|---|
| ermine (41) | etiquette (41) | vexed (42) | insubordination (44) |
| minister (46) | ambassador (47) | conceited (47) | tippler (50) |
| dejection (50) | lugubrious (50) | | |

## Discussion Questions

1. Analyze the narrator's summation of kings: "To them, all men are subjects" (p. 41). (*Kings or other rulers see everyone beneath them as subservient to royalty. They view everyone not as an individual but as a subject who is to obey orders without hesitancy. pp. 41-47*)

2. Examine the author's view of pride and ego as portrayed by the king. (*His pride demands absolute obedience, even if he has to countermand his own orders to fit the time or season. The author views the self-absorbed, ego-filled monarch with disdain, creating an amusing caricature of a king who will do anything to maintain his power. pp. 41-47*)

3. Analyze the irony of the following situations:

   (a) the king's offer to appoint the prince as Minister of Justice (*Since there is no one to judge, the king tells the prince that he can judge an old rat that he hears but does not see. The prince can condemn the rat to death but must then pardon him each time as he is the only "subject" to be judged. If the rat dies, there is no one left to judge, and the prince can no longer administer "justice." pp. 46-47*)

   (b) the conceited man's desire to be admired as the handsomest, best-dressed, richest, and most intelligent man on his planet (*He is the only man on his planet. pp. 49-50*)

   (c) the tippler's shame (*He drinks so that he can forget that he is ashamed of his drinking. pp. 51-52*)

### Supplementary Activities

1. Have students draw a caricature of the king, the conceited man, or the tippler.

2. Assign students the following journal entry: Agree or disagree with the statement, "Conceited people never hear anything but praise" (p. 48). Support your opinion with examples or imaginary scenarios.

## Chapters 13-15, pp. 52-66

The stories of the Little Prince's interplanetary travel continue, including his encounters with the businessman, the lamplighter, and the geographer.

### Vocabulary

| | | | |
|---|---|---|---|
| balderdash (53) | peevishly (55) | lamplighter (57) | voluminous (62) |
| geographer (62) | ephemeral (65) | | |

### Discussion Questions

1. Discuss the irony of the businessman's "matters of consequence" and the prince's reaction to him. *(The businessman spends all his time counting and recounting the stars and thinks he is rich because he "owns" them; therefore, his wealth allows him to buy more stars to count and recount. He has no time for pleasure in life because he is so busy. pp. 52-57)*

2. Examine the futility of the lamplighter's profession and the Little Prince's reaction to him and his planet. *(He lights the one lamp each evening on a planet that has no other people and not one house. The planet has changed, making a complete turn every minute, but the orders to light the lamp each turn have not changed; therefore, he has to light the lamp once every minute. The Little Prince thinks the lamplighter is the only one he has met who does not seem ridiculous. Although he never gets any rest, he remains true to his "calling." The prince hates to leave this planet because it has 1,440 sunsets. pp. 57-62)*

3. Discuss the geographer's work, his view of "eternal things," and the significance of the prince's visit with him. *(He never explores for himself but records in voluminous books only those things others report to him, believing himself to be very important. He doesn't even know anything about his own planet. He records only things that do not change, such as mountains, and is not interested in anything that is in danger of disappearing; therefore, he cares nothing for people or beautiful plants. This visit and talk of ephemeral things reminds the prince of his flower, and he feels his first moment of regret. pp. 62-66)*

### Supplementary Activities

1. Have students write an acrostic for the businessman or the lamplighter. Instructions: place the letters of the word vertically on the paper, then write a word or phrase that describes the character, beginning with each letter.

2. As a class, choose one thing that is eternal and one that is ephemeral, then write a diamente poem contrasting the two things. Pattern—Line 1: one word (noun, the subject); Line 2: two words (adjectives describing line 1); Line 3: three words ("-ing" or "-ed" words that relate to

line 1); Line 4: four words (first two nouns relate to line 1; second two nouns to line 7); Line 5: three words ("-ing" or "-ed" words that relate to line 7); Line 6: two words (adjectives describing line 7); Line 7: one word (noun that is the opposite of line 1). Place lines in the shape of a diamond.

# Chapters 16-19, pp. 66-76
The Little Prince arrives on Earth and first meets the snake. His encounter with a flower and his experience with the echo remind him of his flower.

## Vocabulary
veritable (67)          colleague (68)

## Discussion Questions
1. Describe the Little Prince's first day on Earth. *(He is surprised not to see any people and is afraid he has come to the wrong planet. A snake appears and assures him he is on Earth, in Africa. During their conversation, the prince tells him of his trouble with his flower, and the snake offers to help him return to his own planet when he is ready. pp. 70-74)*

2. Analyze the snake and why he speaks in riddles. *(The snake symbolizes death, and his entwining himself around the prince's ankle reflects his power over him. Death is the answer to each of his riddles; i.e., his power over kings, his ability to carry the prince away from everything, his ability to send all men back to the earth, and his ability to help the prince return to his own planet. pp. 70-74)*

3. Examine the prince's perspective of Earth and correlate with the limited perspective with which we often view other "worlds." *(He thinks the Earth strange: dry [the desert], pointed [the mountain], harsh and forbidding [no one around], people with no imagination [the flower's view of men], and its inhabitants repeat only what they hear [the echo]. pp. 74-76)*

## Supplementary Activities
1. Examine the literary devices: **Similes**—movements of army like those of ballet in the opera (p. 67); he [snake] twined himself around the little prince's ankle, like a golden bracelet (p. 72); peaks of rock sharpened like needles (p. 76) **Metaphor**—snake: coil of gold (p. 70)

2. Assign students the following journal response: Based on the snake's statement, "It is also lonely among men" (p. 72), explain how it is possible to be lonely in the midst of a crowd. This can be poetry or prose.

3. Have students read the biblical account of the snake's approach to Eve in the Garden of Eden (Genesis 3:1-7) and compare with the Little Prince's first encounter with the snake.

4. As a class, write a limerick about the snake.

## Chapters 20-23, pp. 76-90

Through his meeting with the roses, the prince understands that his flower is a rose and is not the only one of her kind. The fox appears as he is weeping over his discovery and teaches him the true meaning of friendship. (Reading aloud the poetic dialogue between the fox and the prince, pp. 83-88, enhances this section.)

### Vocabulary

| | | | |
|---|---|---|---|
| abodes (76) | thunderstruck (77) | perplexed (81) | rites (84) |
| quench (89) | computations (90) | | |

### Discussion Questions

1. Examine the Little Prince's sadness when he learns the true identify of his flower. Correlate with human desire to be unique in some area of life. *(Learning that his flower is just like others makes him feel that his life is common, and he no longer feels princely or rich. Many humans desire to be different. Elicit student response concerning methods by which teenagers seek to be unique and not just "one of the crowd." pp. 76-78)*

2. Analyze the fox's perspective of "taming" one another and its impact on the prince. Discuss the importance of mutual need in a relationship. *(The fox symbolizes trust and friendship. He tells the prince that, in order for them to be friends, the prince must "tame" him; i.e., establish ties. They must mutually need each other, then they will be unique to each other. He explains that "taming" takes time and patience, that they will become responsible for each other, and that, even in the sorrow of their separation, memories of each other will remain. This discourse helps the prince understand why his relationship with his rose is unique: he has cared for her, listened to her, "tamed" her as his own, and is responsible for her. pp. 78-88)*

3. Discuss why the author inserts Chapters 22 and 23 (the railway switchman and the merchant). *(These chapters contrast with the emotion of the exchange between the fox and the prince and point out the things that are lost as people rush about, attempting to save time, and never taking time to develop true friendships. The Little Prince comments that only children know what they are really looking for. pp. 88-90)*

### Supplementary Activities

1. Assign students the following journal response: Complete the phrase, "Friendship is..." in two or three sentences.

2. Analyze the similes: "If you tame me, it will be as if the sun came to shine on my life" (p. 83); "Yours [the prince's steps] will call me, like music, out of my burrow" (p. 83); train rushed by "with a roar like thunder" (p. 88).

3. Analyze the universality of the following: "Words are the source of misunderstandings" (p. 84); "No one is ever satisfied where he is" (p. 89).

## Chapters 24-25, pp. 91-99

The pilot is desperate to repair his plane as his water supply is depleted. The Little Prince is instrumental in helping him find a well. The prince alludes to his own impending departure (death).

### Vocabulary

immensity (92)    radiation (93)    enchantment (93)    descent (98)

### Discussion Questions

1. Examine the relationship between the pilot and the prince. (*They have become friends, and, when the prince asks the pilot to look for a well, he begins the trek across the desert. The pilot reflects on the loyalty and the fragility of the prince. The pilot experiences a sense of grief, a premonition of the impending death of his little friend. pp. 91-97)*

2. Analyze the significance of the water well. Students may want to compare the section beginning with Little Prince's words, "I am thirsty for this water..." with the reference to living water in John 4:13-15, Bible. (*The water symbolizes the quenching of a thirst beyond the physical. The Little Prince compares his thirst for, and satiation by, the water with his understanding of what he really longs for, his single rose. Symbolically, his search for what is really important in life is nearing an end. pp. 94-97)*

3. Discuss the clues to the impending death of the Little Prince. (*...even if one is about to die... [p. 91]; What I see here is nothing but a shell [p. 93]; the pilot's sense of grief [p. 97]; You have plans that I do not know about [p. 98]; the approaching anniversary of the prince's descent to earth [p. 98])*

### Supplementary Activities

1. Assign students the following journal response: Explain the universality of the phrases "...what gives them their beauty is something that is invisible...What is most important is invisible" (p. 93).

2. Analyze the literary devices: **Similes**—image of a rose that shines...like the flame of a lamp (pp. 93-94); ...as if he himself were a flame (p. 94); pulley moaned like an old weathervane (p. 94); it [water] was as sweet as some special festival treat (p. 96) **Personification**—We have wakened the well, and it is singing (p. 96).

## Chapters 26-27, pp. 99-113

The Little Prince tells the pilot that he is going back home. The snake "assists" him with his poison, and the prince dies. The pilot returns home, reflecting on the impact of the Little Prince on his life.

### Vocabulary

asunder (100)          abyss (102)          resolute (106)

### Discussion Questions

1. Analyze the conversation between the Little Prince and the snake (death), its impact on the pilot, and the result. *(The prince arranges to meet the snake at night in the exact alignment with his planet overhead. He tells the pilot he is going home, that he should not come to see his departure, that they will always be friends, and that he will see him in one of the stars. The pilot returns, the snake bites the prince, and he gently falls. pp. 99-108)*

2. Examine the Little Prince's approach to death. *(He wants the snake to promise him the poison will not make him suffer too long, he is pale and afraid but resolute to return to care for his rose, he reassures the pilot of his everlasting friendship, he vows he will continue to live. pp. 100-107)*

3. Analyze the resolution of the story. *(Six years pass. The pilot experiences a mixture of sorrow and happiness. He did not find the Little Prince's body at daybreak and knows he has returned to his planet and his rose. The pilot is concerned whether or not the sheep has eaten the flower because he failed to draw a muzzle on the sheep. pp. 109-110)*

4. Examine the final picture and analyze why the narrator views it as the "loveliest and saddest landscape in the world." *(Responses will vary. Possible answer: It is lovely because of the star shining just above, reminding the narrator of the Little Prince. It is sad because the landscape itself is empty and he longs to believe that the Little Prince will someday return. pp. 112-113)*

### Supplementary Activities

1. Assign students the following journal response: Examine the phrase "...he was rushing headlong toward an abyss from which I could do nothing to restrain him..." (p. 102). Tell of a time you felt this way about someone you love.

2. Analyze the literary devices: **Similes**—snake let himself flow easily across the sand like the dying spray of a fountain (p. 100); heart beating like the heart of a dying bird...(p. 100); it [the prince's laughter] was like a spring of fresh water in the desert (p. 103); water...like music (p. 103); it [body] will be like old abandoned shell (p. 106); he [prince] fell as gently as a tree falls (p. 108); it [listening to the stars] like five hundred million little bells (p. 109)
**Metaphor**—stars: guides for travelers, lights in sky for some, problems for scholars, wealth for businessman, laughter for pilot (p. 104)

# Post-reading Discussion Questions

1. Analyze the narrator's predicament as the novel opens. Correlate with Saint-Exupéry's biography. *(1,000 miles from habitation, water for only one week, attempting to repair wrecked plane; Saint-Exupéry was a pilot and was stranded and without water in the desert in 1935 after his plane crashed. pp. 5-6)*

2. Place Maslow's Hierarchy of Human Needs on an overhead transparency. Discuss these needs and how they relate to the Little Prince, his travels, and the lessons he learned. *(Responses will vary.)* Needs Chart: (1) Physiological Needs (food, water, oxygen, protection) (2) Safety Needs (protection from harm) (3) Love, Affection, Belonging Needs (give and receive, escape loneliness) (4) Esteem Needs (self-respect, respect from others) (5) Self-actualization Needs (involved outside self-needs, devotion to something precious to individual)

3. Discuss the significance of narrator's statement, "I should have liked to begin this story in the fashion of the fairytales...'Once upon a time...'" (p. 17). Ask students why the narrator thinks this would have given greater air of truth to the story. *(Responses will vary. Point out how easily children believe in fairy tales and how cynical some people become as they grow older.)*

4. Examine why his flower is so important to the Little Prince. What are its characteristics? What does it symbolize to the prince? What does it symbolize to the author? *(The flower is beautiful yet vain. The flower becomes the first thing the prince truly loves and allows into his world, yet her vanity drives him away. In retrospect, he realizes the importance of her love and the importance of accepting her as she is. The author's mother and wife were both beautiful, yet their relationships with him were sometimes erratic.)*

5. Analyze the significance of the fox's statement, "But if you come at just any time, I shall never know at what hour my heart is to be ready to greet you...One must observe the proper rites..." (p. 84) *(Responses will vary. Suggested response: People must not take friendships for granted, expecting the friend to be available at all times and in all circumstances. Anticipation of an expected time together enhances the relationship. Even in friendship, certain standards of conduct are expected.)*

6. Discuss whether the novel appeals more to adults or to children. Ask students to identify other books they read as children from which they learned lessons that help them as teenagers or young adults or that would be enjoyable for different age levels. *(Responses will vary. Mention Gulliver's Travels, The Hobbit, etc.; also movies such as "E.T." or "Mary Poppins")*

7. Analyze whether or not the author intended the book to be an allegory or just a children's fable. Discuss attributes of characters if the book is an allegory and/or the moral lesson if it is a fable. *(Allegorical characters: the narrator: adult searching for childhood innocence; the Little Prince: childhood innocence lost and found; the rose: love, vanity [note duality of beauty and thorns]; the snake: death; the fox: friendship. Fable: teaching lesson of what is truly important in life)*

8. Examine the drawings throughout the book and discuss whether or not they accurately depict the message. *(Responses will vary.)*

9. Discuss ways in which the Little Prince thinks grown-ups are extraordinary. *(failure to take time to enjoy sunsets and other lovely things; being consumed with money and things; doing the same thing the same way year after year; hiding from obvious faults; desire to be obeyed and admired)*

10. Analyze why, if the flower drove the Little Prince away, he wants to return to her. Discuss the adage, "Absence makes the heart grow fonder." Apply to situations with which students are familiar. *(Her faults seem less monumental when he has time to reflect on her love for him. The lesson from the fox about establishing ties and becoming responsible for each other reminds him that he needs his flower and she needs him.)*

11. Use the analysis graphic organizers included in this guide. Place on an overhead transparency and elicit student response.

12. Read aloud the poem, "The Land of Beginning Again" by Louisa Fletcher. Correlate with various characters in the novel.

# Post-reading Extension Activities

## Writing

1. Choose one of the following quotes and respond in a paragraph or a poem, relating the quote to a character or situation in the book.

   (a) Each friend represents a world to us, a world possibly not born until they arrive, and it is only by this meeting that a new world is born. (Anais Nin, *The Diary of Anais Nin*, vol. 1, June 1933)

   (b) A friend is a person with whom I may be sincere. Before him, I may think aloud. (Ralph Waldo Emerson, *Essays: First Series*, "Friendship," 1841)

   (c) But if the while I think on thee, dear friend, All losses are restor'd and sorrows end. (Shakespeare, "Sonnet 30," l. 1)

   (d) Only solitary men know the full joys of friendship. Others have their family; but to a solitary and an exile his friends are everything. (Willa Sibert Cather, *Shadows on the Rock*, bk. III, ch. 5, 1931)

   (e) You never know what life means till you die; Even throughout life, 'tis death that makes life live, Gives it whatever the significance. (Robert Browning, *The Ring and the Book*, bk. XI, "Guido," l. 2373, 1868-1869)

   (f) A good death does honor to a whole life. (Petrarch (1304-1374), *To Laura in Death*, canzone 16)

   (g) Gather therefore the Rose, whilst yet is prime, For soon comes age, that will her pride deflower: Gather the Rose of love, whilst yet is time. (Edmund Spenser, *The Fairie Queen*, canto 12, st. 75, 1590)

   (h) Even memory is not necessary for love. There is a land of the living and a land of the dead and the bridge is love, the only survival, the only meaning. (Thornton Niven Wilder, *The Bridge of San Luis Rey*, last lines, 1927)

   (i) Love is...born with the pleasure of looking at each other, it is fed with the necessity of seeing each other, it is concluded with the impossibility of separation. (Jose Marti, *Amor*, 1881)

   (j) Greater love has no one than this, than to lay down one's life for his friends. (Bible, John 15:13, NKJV)

2. Write a poem beginning with "To Look with the Heart..."

3. Write an epilogue for the novel in which the Little Prince returns to his planet.

4. Write a letter to someone who has touched your life, making you a better person.

5. Write a eulogy for the Little Prince.

## Research

1. Research and write a report about the occupation of France by the Nazis during WWII.

2. Research a current environmental concern and write an essay comparing this with the baobabs.

## Art

1. Create a collage personifying death.

2. Design a symbol that represents a true friend, then write a metaphor that correlates with the symbol.

3. Draw a series of caricatures depicting the characters the Little Prince meets while traveling from planet to planet.

## Viewing/Listening

1. View a film version of *The Little Prince*. The two most well-known versions are an animated short (1979) and a musical (1974). Present an oral report to the class in which you compare and contrast the movie with the book.

2. Select and play background music that enhances your oral reading of an emotional portion of the novel.

# Assessment for *The Little Prince*

Assessment is an ongoing process. The following ten items can be completed during the novel study. Once finished, the student and teacher will check the work. Points may be added to indicate the level of understanding.

Name _____ Date _____

**Student**    **Teacher**

_____    _____    1. Correct your unit quizzes; discuss your answers with others in a small group.

_____    _____    2. Identify seven literary devices in the novel. Write three of your own metaphors and similes.

_____    _____    3. Display or perform your extension project on the assigned day.

_____    _____    4. Write a book review. Use at least ten of the vocabulary words you learned from the novel.

_____    _____    5. As the teacher calls out the names of the characters, write an allegorical description of the character or his or her outstanding attribute.

_____    _____    6. Write two review questions over the novel. As a class, conduct the review.

_____    _____    7. Choose one of the themes (friendship, love, innocence) and explain to the class how the theme is developed in the book.

_____    _____    8. Compare your completed cause and effect charts in a small group (page 11 of this guide).

_____    _____    9. Write a diamente poem contrasting the eternal and the ephemeral.

_____    _____    10. Illustrate a scene or line of dialogue from the novel. Include a caption. In a short paragraph, explain why you chose this particular scene.

# Glossary

## Chapters 1-2, pp. 3-10

1. primeval (3): having to do with the first age or ages; original or ancient

2. pondered (3): considered carefully; thought over

3. consequence (5): importance, distinction

4. intimately (5): familiarly; to know well; closely acquainted

5. apparition (6): supernatural sight or thing; ghost or phantom; the appearing of something strange, remarkable, or unexplained

6. cumbersome (9): hard to manage, clumsy; unwieldy, burdensome

7. indulgently (9): giving in to another's whims or wishes; kindly, agreeably

## Chapters 3-4, pp. 10-19

1. peal (11): loud, long sound; loud ringing of bells

2. impenetrable (11): that cannot be entered, pierced, or passed

3. reverie (11): dreamy thoughts of pleasant things, daydream

4. contemplation (12): the act of looking at or thinking about something for a long time; deep thought, meditation

5. asteroid (13): any one of the thousands of the small celestial bodies that revolve around the sun

6. astronomer (14): a person who studies astronomy (the science of the sun, moon, planets, stars, and all other celestial bodies)

7. forbearance (17): patience; self-control; tolerance

## Chapters 5-7, pp. 19-31

1. catastrophe (19): sudden disaster, calamity, or misfortune

2. inoffensively (21): harmlessly; not arousing objections

3. tedious (23): long and tiring; boring, irksome

4. moralist (23): a person who practices or teaches morality

5. naïve (28): simple in nature; like a child; not sophisticated

6. moment (31): importance, weight, significance, consequence

7. blundering (31): bungling, clumsy

## Chapters 8-9, pp. 31-40

1. coquettish (33): seeking to attract merely to please one's vanity; flirtatious

2. abashed (33): embarrassed, confused; made ashamed

3. vanity (33): excessive pride; conceit about one's appearance; ostentatious display

4. complex (35): intricate, complicated, involved

5. stratagems (37): tricks, devices

6. extinct (38): having died out or come to an end

## Chapters 10-12, pp. 41-52

1. ermine (41): fur of an animal like a weasel, usually white

2. etiquette (41): conventional rules of manner; code of conduct

3. vexed (42): annoyed or distressed

4. insubordination (44): disobedience; resistance to authority; refusal to obey

5. minister (46): person in charge of a department of state; diplomatic representation

6. ambassador (47): a diplomatic official; representative of highest rank sent by one state to another

7. conceited (47): having overabundance of opinion of oneself

8. tippler (50): one who habitually drinks alcohol to excess

9. dejection (50): lack of spirit; feeling cast down

10. lugubrious (50): too sad; overly mournful; sorrowful

## Chapters 13-15, pp. 52-66

1. balderdash (53): idle, senseless talk; nonsense

2. peevishly (55): fretfully, querulously, irritably

3. lamplighter (57): a person employed to light gas-burning street lamps

4. voluminous (62): forming or filling a large book or many books

5. geographer (62): a person who knows much about geography

6. ephemeral (65): short-lived; lasting only for a day or a few days

## Chapters 16-19, pp. 66-76

1. veritable (67): true, real, actual

2. colleague (68): associate; companion in employment

## Chapters 20-23, pp. 76-90

1. abodes (76): homes, dwellings

2. thunderstruck (77): overcome; amazed, astonished

3. perplexed (81): puzzled, bewildered

4. rites (84): formal practices or customs, especially religious

5. quench (89): extinguish, put out, slake

6. computations (90): calculations, reckoning; an amount computed

## Chapters 24-25, pp. 91-99

1. immensity (92): very great size; boundless extent; vastness

2. radiation (93): transmission of heat or light from one body to another

3. enchantment (93): use of magic spells; a magic spell or charm

4. descent (98): coming or going down from a higher to a lower place

## Chapters 26-27, pp. 99-113

1. asunder (100): apart, in pieces

2. abyss (102): very deep gulf or pit

3. resolute (106): determined, resolved; fixed in purpose